Wind

From a *Whisper*
to a
Howl

By Chana Stiefel

CELEBRATION PRESS
Pearson Learning Group

Contents

A Mysterious Wonder

Sometimes, it whispers in your ear. Other times, it howls like a wolf. It can be gentle, but when it's strong, it can be powerful enough to uproot trees, overturn cars, and topple buildings. What is this mysterious wonder? It's wind!

Wind isn't just a wild weather phenomenon. Throughout the ages, people have harnessed the power of the wind to fly kites, turn windmills, and soar in airplanes. Some brave pilots fly into the face of strong hurricane winds to collect data and warn people about upcoming storms. This book will explore some of the many ways people are affected by and use wind.

This tree is being bent by hurricane winds.

3

What Is Wind?

Even though wind is invisible, you probably notice its effects every day. You might watch wind whisk leaves off trees or turn umbrellas inside out. Have you ever wondered what causes wind?

Wind is air in motion. Like water, air flows easily from place to place. The force that makes air move is caused by a change in air pressure. Air pressure is the force of air pushing down on an area or surface. Right now, air is pushing down on you in all directions, but you can't see or feel it.

Molecules, or small units, of air tend to move from an area of high pressure to an area of lower pressure. For example, when you open a jar of pickles, you hear a *thwop!* To keep the pickles fresh, most of the air inside is pumped out. At that point, the contents of the jar are under low pressure. You hear the *thwop* sound when the outside, or higher pressure, air rushes into the jar. In the atmosphere, the movement of air from a high-pressure area to a low-pressure area causes wind.

What causes the differences in air pressure to create wind? The answer has to do with heat.

The Sun's rays heat Earth and all of the air surrounding it. Molecules of warm air move around and spread out more than molecules of cold air do. As warm air expands, its pressure decreases. The warm air rises. Cold air has higher pressure. When cold air sinks, it rushes in to replace the warm, rising air. Air under high pressure then moves to an area of low pressure. *Whoosh!* You've got wind.

The greater the difference in air pressure, the faster the air travels, and the stronger the wind will be. Meteorologists, or weather scientists, describe winds by their speed and direction.

To measure wind speed, scientists, sailors, pilots, and others use a device called an anemometer (an-uh-MAHM-uht-uhr). This device has cups mounted on spokes that spin. When wind blows, the cups catch the wind. A speedometer attached to the cups records the wind speed.

Another way to describe wind is to look at its effects on land. In the early 1800s, Admiral Sir Francis Beaufort of the British Royal Navy devised a scale to measure wind forces based on wind speed in miles per hour (mph).

The Beaufort Wind Scale

Force 0	Calm	Less than 1 mph	Smoke rises; air feels still.
Force 1	Light air	1–3 mph	Wind vanes and flags are still.
Force 2	Light breeze	4–7 mph	Leaves rustle.
Force 3	Gentle breeze	8–12 mph	Leaves move gently.
Force 4	Moderate breeze	13–18 mph	Loose paper blows.
Force 5	Fresh breeze	19–24 mph	Small, leafy trees sway.
Force 6	Strong breeze	25–31 mph	Large branches move.
Force 7	Moderate gale	32–38 mph	Whole trees move.
Force 8	Fresh gale	39–46 mph	Branches tear from trees.
Force 9	Strong gale	47–54 mph	Roof shingles blow off.
Force 10	Whole gale	55–63 mph	Trees snap or uproot.
Force 11	Storm	64–73 mph	Cars overturn; trees are blown a distance; widespread damage.
Forces 12–17	Hurricane	More than 74 mph	Trees uproot; buildings are destroyed; massive devastation.

Floating Dragons, Soaring Diamonds

Imagine that it's a Force 5, or a fresh breeze, day. It's a good day to fly a kite. You might see a dragon kite or a parafoil soaring in the sky.

Kites come in a rainbow of colors and a wide variety of shapes and sizes. All kites depend on one thing to get into the air: wind. They need wind to overcome gravity, Earth's downward pull on all objects. Without wind, your kite is grounded.

Different kites fly best in varying wind conditions. For example, diamond and dragon kites soar in light to medium winds. Box kites and parafoils fly better when the wind picks up speed.

Dragon kite

A beach is a popular place for kite flying because the area can be windy, even when the weather is calm inland. A sea breeze, the breeze blowing in from the ocean to land, is an example of a local wind. Local winds are caused by the unequal heating of Earth's surface over a small area.

Here's how the beach kicks up a kite-friendly breeze: The sea and sand soak up the Sun's warmth at different rates. It takes more energy for the Sun to warm up a body of water than it does to heat an equal area of land. Therefore, the air over the sand becomes warmer than the air over the ocean. The warm air expands and rises, creating a low-pressure area. Cool, higher-pressure air blows inland from the ocean and moves beneath the rising warm air.

You don't have to run into the wind to get your kite up in the air. Stand with your back to the wind, away from trees, buildings, cars, and power lines. While you hold the kite string, have a friend stand several yards away holding the kite. Pull back on the string to give it some tension. With a steady breeze behind you, tug on the string while your friend lets go of the kite. Watch it soar!

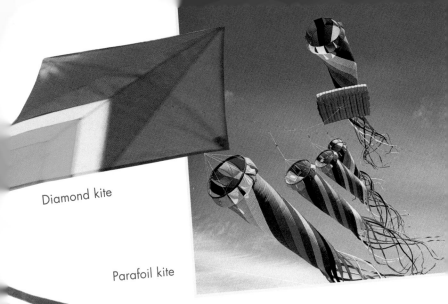

Diamond kite

Parafoil kite

Several forces are at work to keep a kite in the air. For starters, kites get lift, an upward pushing force, from the wind. Kite builders design kites with shapes that are likely to catch the wind and get the most lift.

When the wind blows across the body, or sail, of a kite, the moving air splits into two streams, one above and one beneath the kite. Because of the curved surface of the kite, the air traveling above it moves farther and faster than the flat air stream below it. The difference in air speed is key. As the flow of air speeds up, its pressure drops. That means the air pressure above the kite drops lower, and the higher pressure beneath the kite sends it soaring.

A diamond-shaped kite doesn't climb as high as a parafoil because of its design. The diamond's body is flat instead of curved, so wind doesn't flow smoothly over its surface. Instead, the diamond catches the wind like a sail. This creates a high-pressure zone on its face (the side facing you) and a low-pressure zone behind the kite. The difference in air pressure, from high to low, provides lift.

To keep a diamond-shaped kite in the air, you need to hold it at an angle against the wind. Serious kite fliers call this the angle of attack. In the same way, the sail of a boat needs to face the wind to move a boat forward. In addition, some kites have a tail to provide balance and stability.

With practice, kite flying can be fun for everyone. If you decide to fly a kite, the American Kitefliers Association suggests these safety tips:

- Launch in a wide-open area away from roads, power lines, airports, and trees.
- Never drop the string (also called the line) or reel because the kite can spin out of control.
- Wear gloves to prevent rope burn.
- Never fly a kite in wet or stormy weather because lightning is attracted to wet kite lines.

Kite Career

Kite flying can be a blast. To Colorado researcher Ben Balsley, kites are serious business. For more than a decade, Balsley has been launching huge kites high into the sky to collect scientific data.

Balsley travels around the world to find places with strong, steady winds. In 1990, he launched his first test kites on Christmas Island in the central Pacific Ocean. The two huge kites were each about the size of a tractor-trailer. They soared more than 2 miles high, flying higher than many mountain peaks. Balsley's kites stayed in the air for four straight days collecting weather data.

Hurricane Hunters to the Rescue

If a powerful hurricane was headed your way, would you search for shelter nearby? Would you leave the area? Would you get on an airplane and fly directly into the storm? The first two choices may seem like better ideas, but one group of daredevil pilots chooses to fly into storms.

Hurricane Hunters are members of the Air Force Reserve's Fifty-third Weather Reconnaissance Squadron. They fly through hurricanes to collect weather data. This information tells weather experts if and when a hurricane will reach land. Then, forecasters can tell people how to prepare.

Hurricanes are one of Earth's most harmful storms. Their strength is rated on a scale of 1 to 5. The mildest hurricanes (Category 1) have winds of at least 74 mph. The most violent hurricanes (Category 5) have winds that exceed 155 mph. A Category 5 hurricane can do enormous harm.

During Hurricane Gilbert in 1988, winds gusted up to 218 mph. The hurricane left more than 500,000 people homeless.

No one can stop hurricanes, but the Hurricane Hunters can help prevent the loss of life. During hurricane season, between June and November, they log about 400 hours of flight time.

During these warm months, tropical ocean water heats up. Much of it evaporates and condenses, producing clouds and rain. This process releases even more heat into the air, making it lighter and lowering the air pressure in the center of the storm. More damp air from all around rushes in to replace the rising warm air. Because of Earth's rotation, the air begins to spin, creating high-speed winds. When winds whip above 74 mph, a hurricane is born.

A WC-130 hurricane chaser on a mission.

As a storm starts brewing, satellites signal forecasters at the National Hurricane Center (NHC) in Miami, Florida. Satellites create images of a storm's size and location. To learn precise details about the storm's wind speed and air pressure, forecasters call the Hurricane Hunters.

The crew takes off from their air base. As they fly through the storm, they send wind-speed data every 30 seconds to the NHC. Forecasters use this data to predict the storm's power and direction.

As the crew draws closer to the hurricane's center, the storm becomes increasingly violent. In the eyewall, or the thick ring of clouds that whirls around the storm's center, lightning flashes, winds howl, and rain pounds the aircraft. Soon, the pilots punch through the eyewall into the eye, or the hurricane's quiet center. The wind stops, and the clouds lift. There's an eerie sense of calm.

The Hurricane Hunters have to fly through the eyewall again to get out. The crew crisscrosses the storm three to six times during a 10- to 12-hour mission. They return to their base knowing that the data they collected could save lives. When the next big storm brews over the ocean, these brave pilots will once again face hurricane winds head-on.

Sailing, Sailing . . .

Imagine that you're an explorer who lived 500 years ago. The open sea lies ahead, but you cannot leave the port unless you have one important thing. What would that be? Wind, of course! Sailing ships depend solely on the wind for energy.

From the days of Christopher Columbus through the 1800s, sailors crossing the ocean depended on global winds, which blow steadily in specific directions over long distances. These winds later became known as the trade winds because they enabled European merchants to trade goods with settlers in the New World.

A tall ship uses wind to help it move.

15

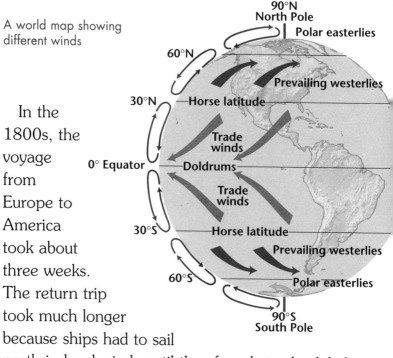

A world map showing different winds

90°N
North Pole
Polar easterlies
60°N
Prevailing westerlies
30°N — Horse latitude
Trade winds
0° Equator — Doldrums
Trade winds
30°S — Horse latitude
Prevailing westerlies
60°S
Polar easterlies
90°S
South Pole

In the 1800s, the voyage from Europe to America took about three weeks. The return trip took much longer because ships had to sail north in local winds until they found steady global winds moving from the northwest to the southeast to carry them home. These winds are called the **prevailing westerlies**.

The trade winds, prevailing westerlies, and other global winds seem to curve toward the right in the Northern Hemisphere. In the Southern Hemisphere, winds curve toward the left. This is because of Earth's rotation. As the winds blow, Earth spins beneath them, making it seem as if the winds curve. This curving motion is known as the **Coriolis effect**.

Sailors try to avoid regions with very little wind. One such zone is called the horse latitudes. Another region with little or no wind lies near the equator, where trade winds from the Northern and Southern Hemispheres meet. Sailors call this region the doldrums. *Doldrums* is a word that also describes the hopeless feeling that sailors have when they become trapped without wind.

Steamships became a more reliable means of transportation for overseas trade than sailing ships. By the late 1800s, steamships began to replace sailing ships. Today, sailing ships are used for recreation rather than trade.

In fact, sailing is a very popular sport. In the America's Cup Race, sailors from around the world sail around a course to see who can win by mastering the wind. Each boat's crew uses instruments to determine the wind's direction and strength. Throughout the race, the crew adjusts the sails to take advantage of the wind's force.

Sailing downwind means to sail with the wind blowing from behind. Sailing downwind, sailors use a large sail called a spinnaker. They position the spinnaker so that it is at a right angle with the length of the boat. The wind fills the sail like a giant parachute as it pushes the boat forward.

However, the real challenge is sailing upwind, or into the wind. A sailboat can't sail directly into the wind because the wind's force would push it back. Instead, the crew sails the boat in a zigzag pattern toward a certain point. This method, called tacking, is like skating uphill. You can't skate straight up, so you zigzag to the top.

On each tack, the crew lines up the sail almost parallel to the boat. The sail, designed like an airplane wing on its side, splits the wind stream. Faster moving air on the outside of the curved sail

Two sail boats use wind to win a race.

creates a low-pressure area. The higher-pressure air on the inside pushes the boat forward. The crew that can capture the wind by adjusting the boat's sails the fastest will win the America's Cup.

Balloon Flight Around the World

In 1999, Bertrand Piccard and Brian Jones flew nonstop around the world in a hot-air balloon called the *Breitling Orbiter 3*. The force that carried them on this journey was provided solely by the wind. Their journey broke a record.

Pilots who fly hot-air balloons have little control over the balloon's direction. They can make the balloon go up or down by adjusting the amount of hot air, or helium. Helium is a gas that is lighter than air and is used to fill party balloons. To make the balloon go up, the pilots fire up burners that heat the gases. To make the balloon go down, they lower the heat. To travel in a certain direction, they have to find the right winds.

Piccard and Jones used the jet stream for most of their trip. The jet stream is made up of high-speed winds. The winds usually blow west to east about 30,000 feet above Earth's surface. Jet-stream winds don't bump into trees or tall buildings.Therefore, they can blow from 80 mph to speeds faster than most hurricane winds.

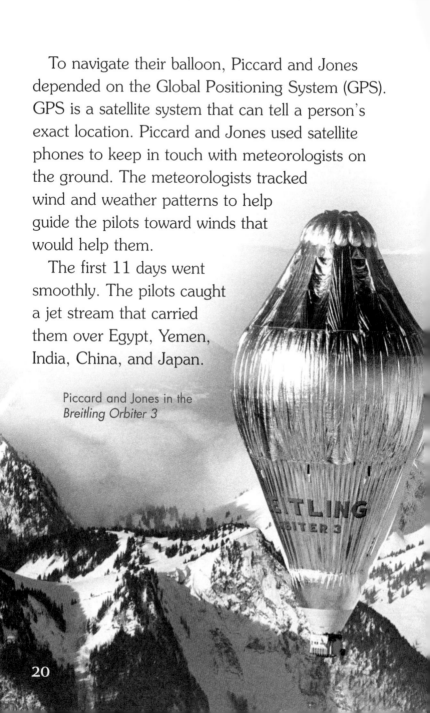

To navigate their balloon, Piccard and Jones depended on the Global Positioning System (GPS). GPS is a satellite system that can tell a person's exact location. Piccard and Jones used satellite phones to keep in touch with meteorologists on the ground. The meteorologists tracked wind and weather patterns to help guide the pilots toward winds that would help them.

The first 11 days went smoothly. The pilots caught a jet stream that carried them over Egypt, Yemen, India, China, and Japan.

Piccard and Jones in the
Breitling Orbiter 3

As the adventurers got close to the Pacific Ocean, they had to decide whether to head north toward faster winds or south to catch slower winds. Storms pounded the north, so forecasters advised the pilots to head south. This added 2,500 miles to the trip.

The voyage over the Pacific was very difficult. While 20 mph winds blew the pilots slowly across the ocean, a broken antenna made them lose communication with their control center. Piccard and Jones lived on freeze-dried food and barely slept. They had to chip ice off the balloon's cables to keep the balloon from crashing.

After six rough days, the weather experts' advice paid off. The *Breitling Orbiter 3* entered a powerful jet stream that carried the balloon quickly over Mexico. However, when the pilots reached the Caribbean, the jet stream changed. The pilots decided to burn lots of fuel to inflate the balloon and climb as high as as possible. Their gas reserves almost hit empty.

High over the Atlantic Ocean, 180 mph winds whisked them to the finish line and into the history books. In Piccard's words, the pilots touched down feeling a "new relationship with our planet—more intimate, more respectful."

Glide Like an Eagle

How would it feel to fly like an eagle? You could ride the wind and soar above mountaintops. People cannot grow wings, but flying in a **glider** might be the next best thing. These aircrafts have no propellers or engines. Instead, glider pilots fly by chasing the invisible forces of rising air currents and wind. Today's technology and designs allow gliders to fly even higher, faster, and farther than the most skilled birds.

To get in the air, glider pilots often hitch a tow with a powered plane. A strong rope connects the two aircrafts as they take off.

When they climb to 2,000 feet, the glider pilot pulls a knob to release the tow rope. The glider is off and soaring!

Gliders are designed to soar a long distance through the air while gravity slowly pulls them down. In 1891, an engineer named Otto Lilienthal became the first person to fly a glider. To control the craft, he shifted his weight from side to side. His gliders looked like today's hang gliders.

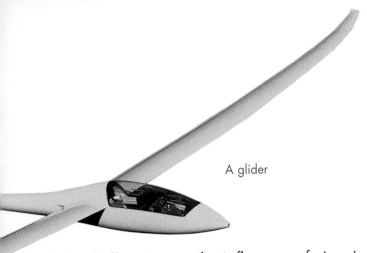

A glider

Lilienthal's notes on the influences of air, wind speed, and weight inspired the brothers Orville and Wilbur Wright to develop improved gliders. As the world's first soaring pilots, they practiced flying on a windy beach at Kitty Hawk, North Carolina. They went on to invent the first pilot-controlled, engine-powered airplane, which took off in 1903.

Today's gliders have wider wingspans than the gliders of the past. Glider wings are gently curved on top. Faster moving air flowing over the top creates a low-pressure area. Higher-pressure air pushing up from below gives the glider lift.

The pilot uses a rudder and wing and tail flaps to steer a sailplane. A sailplane is a light glider. Even if the pilot doesn't catch an uplifting wind, a sailplane starting at 2,000 feet can drift through air for at least ten minutes.

The big challenge and thrill of glider flight is for the pilot to find winds and air currents that lift the aircraft high into the sky. One lifting force is called ridge lift. Pilots find ridge lift near the slopes of mountains or hills.

When the wind blows against the side of a mountain, the airflow is pushed upward. The flowing air can rise hundreds of feet above the top of the ridge. Gliders can fly back and forth for hours in this rising wind. Some pilots can fly as many as 1,000 miles riding the ridge lift along mountain ranges.

For a really exciting ride, glider pilots also aim for a powerful kind of lift called wave lift. Wave lift occurs when winds with speeds of 25 mph or more blow at a right angle to the side of a mountain or ridge. The wind flows over the top of the mountain and down the other side. Then it "bounces" off stable air near the ground and shoots up thousands of feet to another area of stable air. There, it turns downward again, making a glider ride seem like a bumpy roller coaster.

Gliders can climb at a rate of 2,000 feet per minute or more on the rising side of each wave. Above 12,500 feet, glider pilots need oxygen masks to breathe.

You don't need mountains or ridges to catch lifting air currents. Sometimes, all you need is an asphalt parking lot or flat, rocky ground. These open areas absorb heat from the Sun and provide another glider boost called thermal lift.

When the Sun heats the ground, hot air bubbles rise up, like steam rising from a boiling kettle. The upward surges of rising air form spiral columns called thermals. In some parts of the United States, glider pilots have risen in thermals as high as 18,000 feet.

To find thermals, glider pilots look for puffy cumulus clouds. Thermals form cumulus clouds when the moisture they carry cools and condenses at high altitudes. Pilots may also look for birds circling in midair without flapping their wings. The birds might be riding a thermal updraft.

The sport of soaring has taken off. There are many people who fly gliders worldwide. Training can take one week to two months and may cost $800 to $2,000.

Some fliers try to break world records for altitude, distance, and speed. Others take on the challenge of cross-country racing. Mostly, though, glider pilots fly to soar up to the clouds and enjoy the sights and sensations of riding the wind.

Power Winds

Along the Oregon-Washington border is the Stateline Wind Energy Center, which is a wind farm. Its wind turbines are like high-tech windmills. They harness the wind's energy and use that energy to produce electricity. Stateline is one of the largest wind farms in the world. Its turbines provide enough electricity to power 70,000 homes and businesses.

How does an invisible force such as wind provide power? Steady winds of 5 mph or more spin the rotor of a wind turbine. The rotor is a set of large rotating blades.

Wind Turbine

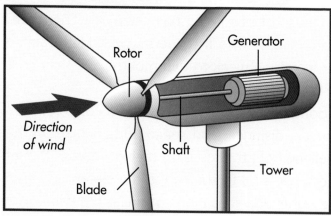

Rotor

Generator

Direction of wind

Shaft

Tower

Blade

The rotor captures the wind's energy of motion. Moving air has mechanical energy. Mechanical energy is the ability to do work. As the rotor spins, it turns a shaft. The shaft then drives an electric generator, which turns the wind's mechanical energy into electricity. Many wind farms are connected to large companies that supply electricity to areas that need it. The largest rotors used to produce electricity for wind farms are 200 feet or more.

Rotors are usually at the top of high towers. This is because winds are usually stronger high above the ground, where there are no obstacles in the way. Some towers are 165 feet high.

Experts say that wind energy is the world's fastest growing source of power. The world now uses ten times as much wind energy as it did ten years ago. Today, millions of homes all over the world depend on wind energy for power.

Europe is the world leader in wind-energy production. It makes 70 percent of the world's wind power. Denmark is the leading country in wind-energy production, receiving 18 percent of its power from wind. It is followed by Germany and Spain. The trend is picking up speed in the United States.

Wind-farm projects have been started in more than 25 states. However, most homes still do not use wind as their energy source.

Today, when you turn on your computer, the electricity you use most likely comes from fuel-burning power plants. Fossil fuels, such as oil, coal, or natural gas, provide most of the world's energy.

The problem with burning fossil fuels is that they release toxic substances and heat, trapping greenhouse gases in the atmosphere. Once these fuels are burned, they cannot be replaced.

A wind farm

As the world's population grows, these problems could get worse. By some estimates, the use of electricity will rise nearly 70 percent by the year 2020.

These concerns have prompted many countries to explore wind power as another source of energy. Like solar power, wind is a renewable resource. It is continuously renewed by nature, so it will never run out. In addition, wind turbines do not give off any harmful substances.

One problem with wind power is that only certain regions have winds strong and 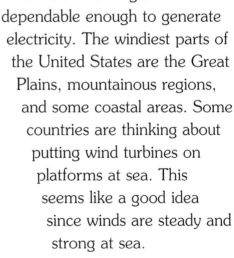 dependable enough to generate electricity. The windiest parts of the United States are the Great Plains, mountainous regions, and some coastal areas. Some countries are thinking about putting wind turbines on platforms at sea. This seems like a good idea since winds are steady and strong at sea.

However, even at the windiest sites, wind speeds vary by time of day and season and from year to year. When winds cannot provide enough electricity, other energy sources must be used.

Another problem is the look of wind farms. Some people think wind turbines look graceful. Others dislike the way wind farms look.

Some people worry about noise from the wind-turbine rotors. Fortunately, modern turbines are quiet. The blades spin slowly, and they are usually not heard above the sound of the wind itself.

Another concern is that wind turbines kill birds that accidentally get caught in the rotor blades. To solve this problem, wind-energy companies are locating sites away from bird migration routes, building towers that prevent nesting, and painting blades to make them more visible.

Wind can be a powerful force, even though it is invisible. Today, wind power and other new renewable resources provide only a small percentage of the world's energy needs. Maybe you can think of new ways to harness wind for energy. Increasing the use of wind power won't be a breeze, but it will be well worth the effort!

- The highest wind speed ever recorded on Earth blew across Mount Washington in New Hampshire on April 12, 1934. It measured more than 200 mph. Buildings on the mountain today are anchored by chains.

- A chinook, a warm wind that blows down the eastern slope of the Rocky Mountains, can melt snow in a few hours.

- The windchill factor measures the cooling effect of wind. The stronger the wind and the lower the air temperature, the bigger the chill. The windchill factor explains why a 20 degree day, with 30 mph winds, can feel like 18 degrees below zero.

- Neptune is the planet that has the fastest winds in the solar system. They reach speeds of up to 1,200 mph. The winds may be caused by heat escaping the planet's interior.

- In the continental United States, the city with the highest average wind speed is Amarillo, Texas.

Glossary

air pressure — the force of air pushing down on an area or surface

anemometer — a device that measures wind speed

Beaufort Wind Scale — a chart that describes winds by their effects on land

Coriolis effect — the manner in which Earth's rotation makes global winds curve toward the right or left

glider — an aircraft designed to fly without propellers or an engine; kept in the air by wind and rising air currents

global winds — winds that blow steadily from specific directions over long distances

jet stream — bands of high-speed winds that blow west to east about 30,000 feet high in the atmosphere

lift — an upward pushing force that enables kites, planes, and other heavier-than-air objects to overcome gravity's downward pull

local winds — winds caused by the unequal heating of Earth's surface over a small area

prevailing westerlies — global winds that blow from the northwest to the southeast

windchill — the cooling effect of wind